MW01229663

TEACH ME TO READ, WRITE and THINK

STEP G: Learn what a syllable is, how to divide words into syllables, and which syllable is usually stressed or accented for decoding longer words

Rebecca Stone

ISBN-10: 1481173871

ISBN-13: 978-1481173872

Table of Contents

A baby does not learn to talk in a room with twenty-five other babies and one adult. He/she learns to talk in a one on one relationship with an adult or older child, and learns a multitude of sounds and words quickly.

Reading is best taught in a one on one situation. The younger the child the easier it is for the child to learn. The "Reading Recovery" program used very early is the latest and most efficient way to teach children experiencing difficulty in reading in public schools. One teacher works with one child thirty (30) minutes daily. Many schools are finding this to be extremely successful. Ideally, all children could be taught in this manner. Needless to say, public funding is not sufficient to do this in all schools, but you can do it at home with YOUR CHILD.

Learning to read should to be FUN and REWARDING. It should not be considered a chore by student or teacher. In a parent-child situation undivided, loving attention is the first reward a child feels. What better reward for a child or parent is there? What better recreation is there than reading or being read funny, ridiculous, suspenseful, or true to life stories and poems?

Encouraging words, smiles, pats, hugs, and kisses are a MUST. Use them often but sincerely. Children know when you are not honest with them. Use such expressions as, "You know that letter or sound. You read that sentence. You can read this page very well. You can write or tell an interesting sentence or story. I really enjoyed listening to you read today. I had fun with you today. I'm so proud of you. I love you very much."

....

Consistency is of utmost importance in accomplishing any task. A certain time, place, and attitude for working with your child would be most desirable, but in today's world this probably is not achievable for most parents and children. This does not mean you cannot accomplish just as much, but more thought and priority must be given to scheduling and planning this most important activity.

Thirty minutes more or less should be planned in your schedule five days each week. This does not mean that you should not work more than five days if interest and time permit. Likewise some weeks will not permit working five days for the obvious reasons of illness, being out of pocket for business and other necessary and unavoidable reasons. Do not feel that these times are disastrous to your reading program. Think of them as a little "vacations" and begin again as soon as possible with a positive and joyful attitude. The best part of a vacation is getting back home and into a regular routine.

Consistency of place in most cases will probably be the easiest part to accomplish. It needs to have the least distraction possible such as noise, activity, and other persons. It can be a table or spot on the floor of a corner in the quietest room available. The more privacy you share with your child the more your child will feel special. The more special your child feels the more you will accomplish in reading. If possible for variety you may change the spot from time to time. On warm sunny days it may be fun to work outdoors. The activity you are doing should be considered when making a change in place. If you are writing sentences, short stories, or just looking for words that have a certain beginning or ending sound, a trip to other parts of the house, outdoors, or even a short walk or trip in the car could be motivating and a fun change.

Both parent and child need to have a "want to" attitude to make the most of their reading time. You should feel relatively healthy, rested, fed, and in a fairly congenial mood. Sometimes you will have little control over how rested or healthy you are, and sometimes you or your child will have had a bad day. At these times you may want just to rest with each other, hold your child and talk about the day. Later you may want to write and read a sentence or two about feelings or read a favorite book together. Most children and adults do not get enough rest. All children need at least ten hours of sleep nightly. Hunger will probably be the easiest problem to solve. Eat together! Have fun! Write and read words about food and eating.

The more you enrich and expand a child's daily activities the more his speaking, reading and writing vocabulary will expand. Do a totally new or different activity with your child as often as possible. Talk with your child and listen to him/her talk as you share in the activity. You should point out and discuss related words but don't make it a "lesson". Make it as fun and memorable as possible. As with adults, the child will enjoy some activities and dislike others. That's OK. Learning still takes place. If you think the activity is especially beneficial, try it several times. Your child will probably learn to enjoy it. It may be like a disliked food that when eaten several times begins to taste better.

To enrich and expand your child's experiences try some of the following activities: Draw, paint, listen to different music, cook, build, sew, fish, garden outside or in a pot. Play and attend new games and sports. Visit museums, art galleries, concerts, plays, shows (some are free), zoos, specialty stores, churches, different age or ethnic groups and restaurants.

Try different modes of travel and vacation in a totally different environment: large city, small town, rural settings, farms, ranches, deserts, rain forest (There are some in the U.S.), mountains, plains, etc.

It may not be feasible for you to travel, visit museums, zoos, theaters or concert halls, but books can offer much enrichment. Read yourself and read to your child daily. Have as many and as great a variety of books and magazines available to your child as you can afford to buy or borrow. Garage sales and thrift stores area an economical sources and libraries are free.

Read and discuss with your child the information, experiences and feelings that the books and magazines offer. There are excellent magazines published for all age children such as Cricket and National Geographic Magazines.

Monitored and sparingly used television programs of the Public Broadcasting System and C-Span, travel and science programs can be a great source of enrichment. Sesame Street can certainly help with teaching the alphabet, numbers, colors, etc. Use television wisely and minimally.

Overview of Book and Teaching Methods

This book is designed as a nuts and bolts approach to teaching reading, writing and thinking to a young child, or an older child having problems with these skills. All the language skills presented in this book could be useful in teaching older students as well as adults by making modifications in the presentation and activities.

Reading is taught by using a phonics approach to decoding words. Phonics is simply the sound that the letters or groups of letters of the alphabet make. Once these patterns and their sounds are learned, any word can be decoded (sounded out). These phonics skills are taught by using a step by step process. How to teach these steps is clearly and thoroughly explained using simple materials and activities. Follow the steps in sequential order. Some steps take longer than others.

Children do not like tests and adults like them even less. The word TEST should NEVER be mentioned. Most steps have an evaluation sheet or activity. If you use these, it should be done in a very casual way with no importance insinuated to the child. These are for the comfort level of some parents. You will know how your child is progressing by working with him. If the child performs at 75% to 80% on the activity, you may skip the step or go to the next step.

In a public school setting where one teacher is responsible for 25 to 30 students, these steps take much longer. In a one on one teaching setting depending on the motivation and interest of the learner and teacher, they can take a fraction of the time. Do not be concerned about the time a step takes as long as your child and you are enjoying the activities and making some progress. Do not stay on a step too long. Your child does not have to be perfect. Move on to another step or activity. DO NOT BORE YOUR CHILD! You will be reviewing and using all the skills in the next step. Just for your information an approximate time line of the speed these skills are taught in most public schools is included. You will see that you are moving much, faster.

Writing and reading go together. When a word is learned, it can be used to write. Writing reinforces reading skills and reading reinforces writing skills. The two should be taught together.

Words will be written as simple lists, (ball, tall, hall, wall), couplets (blue ball), phrases (under the table) and sentences (The blue ball rolled under the table.), and stories (Tom's dad bought him a new, blue ball. Tom liked the ball. Tom and Dad played with the ball.

Tom rolled the ball to Dad in the hall. Dad missed the ball. The blue ball rolled under the table. Tom crawled under the table to get the ball. Dad and Tom had fun playing with the new, blue ball.)

Spelling occurs when a word is written. Each time a word is written, the spelling of the word is reinforced. The more a child writes the better speller the child becomes. Very young children who love to write do not worry about spelling. Have the child read to you what he/she has written. You will catch the spelling errors but do not point them out until the writing has been shared and enjoyed. If and when you help the child edit the writing, point out the misspelled words by saying, "You are really a great inventive speller. I could read every word, but I know you want to learn to spell them correctly."

When the child writes a word he/she has chosen to convey an idea, that word is more likely to be internalized and spelled correctly again than one memorized for a test. The only spelling test a child should have is when he/she edits his/her own writing.

As you teach phonetic principles for sounding out words, you are teaching spelling. The knowledge of phonetic principles is the best tool for producing accurate spellers. This tool plus writing far outweighs the benefit of any spelling text or word list. Phonetics is spelling.

Encourage the child to write about things and activities he/she considers to be fun. Provide opportunities to promote writing for FUN. Writing improves spelling and reading more than any other activity. The more a child writes the better he/she spells. Like any other acquired skill, practice is the key.

Thinking skills should also be taught with reading and writing skills. Thinking is taught simply by asking questions about what is read, and discussing the responses. Ask questions recalling details such as time, place, things, names, events, etc. Questions about details usually have a correct or incorrect answer. Questions about feelings, attitudes, actions, purposes, accomplishments, and consequences on the other hand may have more than one correct answer. These questions require probing and discussion which is the true basis for teaching thinking skills. Ask questions such as How did the characters feel? Did the feelings change? Why do you think feelings did or did not change? How would you have felt? Why did the characters act as they did? Did the actions of the characters accomplish something, help someone, hurt someone, make someone happy or sad? Do you think the characters should have acted in a different way? Did the story have a satisfactory ending? Would you have ended the story in the same way? How would you change the beginning or ending of the story? *Work to become an expert on asking thought provoking questions and giving positive feedback on all responses.* You will be teaching your child critical reading and thinking skills.

As stated in the first paragraph of the introduction, this book is designed to teach young children beginning about ages three or four. It uses a phonetics based approach combined with whole language (speaking, listening, writing and reading). It begins by teaching recognition of the letters of the alphabet, sounds of letters and combination of letters to make words. Some hold to the theory that very young children even newborn babies, can learn to read by being shown whole words. It certainly would not hinder a child if he/she were shown neatly written words that named objects, people, activities or feelings in his/her environment, experience, or interest level. Books, signs, papers, magazines, etc., constantly present sight words. Use them. They can only enhance reading skills. As phonetic skills are learned, these familiar sight words might be used to illustrate a phonetic principle or its exception. As with an older child, the more exposure to words, the better.

A basic sight words list is included in Step C Resource Section with the suggestion to make flash cards to check the child's recognition of the words and/or to use for needed drill for those words needing more practice.

Always begin and/or end each session by reading for enjoyment with your child. Reading at the end of the session may be for enjoyment of the child's writing or for practice and review. **Don't forget to ask thought provoking questions that begin with, "Why..? What do you think..? What would you do..? How did he feel..? How would you feel..?" etc.**

Learn what a syllable is, how to divide words into syllables, and which syllable is usually stressed or accented for decoding longer words

REMINDERS AND TIPS

Listen.   **Discuss.**   **Ask probing questions.**

Give positive feedback on all answers to questions and work. "That is right. You made an excellent guess or try. You were a diligent worker today."

Read to the child a book or part of a book each day.

Keep a large selection of children's books available. Go to the library weekly. Give and ask for books for gifts. Yard sales are an excellent source of reasonably priced books.

Have the child read to you each day a selection from "I Can Read and Write" and another book.

Do you need to review vowel sounds in Step C? **Vowel sounds are the key to decoding and spelling words.**

Ask the child to select one of the writings in "I Can Read and Write" which has not been edited, and ask him to edit it without help. Before he/she begins quickly review things to keep in mind such as capital letters, end punctuation, spelling. After the editing give positive feedback and suggestions for improvement if necessary. Was one word used too frequently, or would some describing words or different action words improve a sentence? This activity can serve as an indicator for review or more practice.

Congratulations! You have successfully completed six of the seven steps. You and your child deserve a GREAT BIG REWARD! Plan something extraordinary that you both will enjoy immensely and remember forever.

Overview, Materials List, Evaluation

OVERVIEW

All words are made up of one or more parts. Each **vowel sound** makes one part or **syllable**. A syllable may have two vowels, but they make only one sound. A syllable is determined by one vowel sound not by how many vowels you see. Two vowels can combine to make only one vowel sound as in (feet). You see two vowels but hear only one vowel sound so the word has only one syllable.

Knowing how to divide words into syllables is a useful decoding skill. If a two, three, or more syllable word can be broken into parts with one vowel sound each, it can be decoded by putting the three sounds together. The following activities will give general patterns or clues for dividing unknown words into parts for decoding purposes. There are few hard, fast rules with no exceptions in dividing words, but most words follow patterns. These patterns are helpful guides.

MATERIALS LIST

Papers—regular lined notebook or copy of line paper in the resource section, 3x5" cards, "I Can Read and Write" and "Words I Know" books
Markers—medium, dark felt tip, highlighter
Pencils—regular # 2 lead
Other—scissors

EVALUATION

There are review and evaluation activities for these skills at the end of the section. They may be used to assess the child's skill level before or after working on an activity.

Dividing Compound Words Into Syllables

The first and simplest way to teach syllabication (si .lab'i .ka' shun) the act of dividing words into syllables, is to use compound words made with **two one-syllable words**. Write the following compound words on 3x5" cards leaving a little more than average space between letters so that the word can be cut into two parts.

b a c k p a c k   p o p c o r n

g o l d f i s h   d o g h o u s e

b a s e b a l l   m y s e l f

a i r p l a n e   r a i n c o a t

m a i l b o x   s n o w f a l l

p e a n u t   c u p c a k e

Ask the child to read the word and tell you the two vowel sounds heard. Then ask him/ her to divide the word into two parts by cutting between the two words. Say, "You have divided a two syllable word into its two parts. Each part has one vowel sound. What is the vowel sound in each part? What letter (s) made the sound?"

Vowel-Consonant / Consonant-Vowel (VC•CV) Pattern

The next easiest principle is that **two consonants between two vowels are usually divided between the two consonants.** Show the child the following lists of words. Both lists have two consonants between two vowels.

In List 1 both consonants are the same and are more easily spotted, but point out that the consonants do not have to be the same. Ask child to highlight the double consonants in each word and then draw a vertical line between them. Say, "You have divided the word into its two syllables. What is the vowel sound in each syllable? Say the word." Ask the child to choose 5–10 words from each list to write in "Words I Know" book.

List 1: Like Consonants

1. ki**t**ten	8. buddy*	15. offer
2. cotton	9. daddy	16. motto
3. kennel	10. gossip	17. lesson
4. rabbit	11. effort	18. ladder
5. pillow	12. carry	19. muffin
6. letter	13. dollar	20. mirror
7. butter	14. happy	

List 2: Unlike Consonants

1. nu**m**ber	8. grumpy	15. whisper
2. window	9. after	16. pencil
3. absent	10. citron	17. perfect
4. basket	11. plenty*	18. kidney
5. garden	12. picnic	19. object
6. fifty*	13. person	20. magnet
7. goblin	14. winter	

*(Y) is a vowel at the end of a word. It makes the (long e) sound at the end of a two or more syllable word.

Dividing Words with (-le)

Another easy pattern is dividing words ending in (-le). **The consonant letter before the (-le) goes with it to make the last syllable of the word.** The vowel sound is a short (u) sound as in the word up (candle — can•dle).

Show the following list of words and ask the child to draw a vertical line to show that the consonant before the (-le) goes with it to make the last syllable of the words. Have him/her say the vowel sound in each syllable and then say the word putting the two sounds together.

Exception: When (-le) is preceded by (ck), as in pickle and tickle, the (-le) form a separate syllable (pick•le, tick•le).

1. a ble
2. ankle
3. bugle
4. cable
5. circle
6. cradle
7. double
8. idle
9. gentle
10. fumble
11. sta ble*
12. rustle
13. jungle
14. kindle
15. noodle
16. maple
17. bridle
18. people
19. turtle
20. table

*A vowel at the end of a syllable is long. In sta•ble, vowel (a) is long, says its name.

Dividing Words with Vowel-Consonant-Vowel (VCV) Pattern

In a word with the vowel-consonant-vowel (VCV) pattern, the consonant usually goes with the second vowel to form a syllable. Show the child the following words and explain the V•CV pattern.

VCV	V•CV
bacon	ba•con
open	o•pen

Reminder: A vowel at the end of a syllable is usually long.

Help the child complete the following chart. Say each syllable and word. Ask him/her to choose 5–10 words to write in "Words I Know" book.

VCV	*highlight VCV*	*divide into syllables*
meter	meter	me ̣ter *
polite	polite	po ̣lite **
cider	_____	_____
began	_____	_____
bacon	_____	_____
below	_____	_____
direct	_____	_____
divide	_____	_____
erase	_____	_____
paper	_____	_____
pilot	_____	_____
tiger	_____	_____

zero   _____   _____

obey   _____   _____

over   _____   _____

favor   _____   _____

meter   _____   _____

Words for additional practice:

open, vacant, even, lazy, lilac, fever,

soda, silent, pupil, story, music

*The vowel at the end of a syllable is usually long.

**This vowel (o) in the first syllable makes the schwa sound (same as a short u) as in up.
A vowel often makes this sound in an unaccented syllable.

Exceptions to V•CV Principle

The V•CV principle that a consonant between two vowels usually goes with the second vowel is less consistent than previous principles. **When the consonant is put with the second vowel, it makes the first vowel long because it is at the end of a syllable or is alone.**

V•CV	**V•CV**
be•long	e•rase

Sometimes this division will not make a word. Look at the following divisions. Which makes a word?

V•CV		**VC•V**
se•ven	*or*	sev•en
sa•vage	*or*	sav•age

The first division of each does not make a word because the letters (e) and (a) in the first syllables would make a long sound. The second division (VC•V) makes the vowels short and makes the word.

Say the words with the long vowel sound in the first division. Does it sound like a word? Then say the words with the short sound in the second division. It sounds like a word. Children like to do this. It is also good review of when a vowel is long and short.

Note: In words of more than one syllable, the letter (v) usually goes with the preceding vowel to form a word. Examples of words where the letter (v) goes with the preceding vowel are:

nev•er   trav•el   riv•er   clev•er   shiv•er   giv•en

To divide words with the (VCV) pattern, first divide the word by putting the C with the second V (V•CV). This makes the first vowel long. If it does not sound like a word, divide it by putting the C with the first vowel (VC•V) making the first vowel short.

Show the following words with the two divisions, sound them out and ask the child
"Which sounds like a word?" The first division makes the first vowel long and second
division makes the first vowel short.

	V•CV	**VC•V**
1. metal	me•tal (long e—eat)	met•al (short e—egg)
2. liver	li•ver (long i—pie)	liv•er (short i—it)
3. magic	ma•gic (long a—ate)	mag•ic (short a—at)

Continue now or later for more practice with this pattern.

	V•CV	**VC•V**
4. logic	lo•gic	log•ic
5. medal	me•dal	med•al
6. memo	me•mo	mem•o
7. melon	me•lon	mel•on
8. model	mo•del	mod•el
9. modest	mo•dest	mod•est
10. solemn	so•lemn	sol•emn
11. monarch	mo•narch	mon•arch

Sometimes a word can be divided both ways to make two different words.

12. minute	mi•nute	min•ute
	meaning very small	meaning 60 seconds

Endings, Prefixes and Suffixes

A prefix, suffix or ending with a vowel sound makes a syllable. Show the child and discuss how the following words are divided into syllables, pointing out the syllables that are made with prefixes, suffixes, and endings. Say the vowel sound in each syllable.

Endings

boxes — box·es

dishes — dish·es

printed — prin·ted*

rested — res·ted*

parking — park·ing

helping — help·ing

waded — wa·ded*

needed — nee·ded*

Prefixes

repack — re·pack

unlock — un·lock

disobey — dis·o·bey

subway — sub·way

rewrite — re·write

unbutton — un·button

displeased—dis· pleased

submarine—sub·ma·rine

Suffixes

useful — use·ful

sleepless — sleep·less

gladly — glad·ly

longer — long·er

playful — play·ful

thickness — thick·ness

slowly — slow·ly

fastest — fast·est

*(-ed) is **not a syllable** if it makes the (d) or (t) sound. It **is a syllable** after words ending with the letter (t) or (d) and makes the (id) sound.

Copy the following list of words. Ask the child to practice dividing the following words into syllables with a marker. Give assistance if needed.

1. un:safe	11. dislike
2. tallest	12. hopeful
3. painful	13. thickness
4. floated	14. gladly
5. retell	15. sleepless
6. players	16. talking
7. unhappy	17. sounded
8. harmless	18. reuse
9. cheerful	19. untied
10. disable	20. lighted

Dividing Words with Consonant Blends

When the first vowel in a word is followed by a consonant blend, the blend usually begins the second syllable. Show the child the following list of words. Review with the child the principle for dividing words into syllables that says:

When the first vowel in a word is followed by a consonant, the consonant often goes with the second vowel to make the second syllable.

Tell the child that the following words have a consonant blend after the first vowel. If needed, review consonant blends by looking at beginning activities in Step D. *Consonant blends are not divided to make syllables.*

Copy the following list. Ask the child to highlight or underline the consonant blend following the first vowel. Then divide the word into syllables. Do not divide between the two consonants of a blend or digraph.

example: across—a⋮**cr**oss

1. apron	8. ostrich
2. asleep	9. degree
3. reply	10. defrost
4. secret	11. abridge
5. problem	12. instruct
6. describe	13. entrench
7. agree	14. program

When a consonant is followed by a consonant blend, the blend usually begins the second or next syllable.

Copy the following words. Point out the consonant followed by a consonant blend. Ask the child to highlight the blend and then divide the word between the first consonant and the consonant blend.

example: complex—com|**pl**ex

1. ingredient
2. construct
3. surprise
4. hungry
5. hundred
6. monster
7. hamster
8. concrete

9. complain
10. control
11. laundry
12. farther
13. address
14. improve
15. instant
16. explains

Review Principles of Syllabication

Go over each principal give example as a review of syllabication. Ask child,
"What is a syllable?" **A syllable is each part of a word having one vowel sound.**
If a vowel makes a sound, it can be a syllable by itself. It may have other silent vowels
and consonants with it as one syllable. **Some principles for dividing
words into syllables:**

1. Divide between words in a compound word made up of two
   1-syllable words.

   pop·corn, rain·coat, gold·fish, cup·cake, my·self

2. Divide between two consonants between two vowels (VC·CV).
   Consonants may be the same or not the same. Like consonants are
   easier to spot.

   le**t·t**er, pu**p·p**y, wi**n·t**er, pe**r·s**on

3. The letters (-le) at the end of a word combine with the preceding
   consonant to make the last syllable of the word.

   jun·**gle**, cir·**cle**, bu·**gle**, gen·**tle**

4. If a word has a vowel, consonant, vowel pattern (VCV), the consonant
   usually goes with the second vowel but not always. If the division
   does not sound like a word, put the consonant with the first vowel.

   V ·CV: ba·**co**n, **o·pe**n, si·**le**nt, **ze·ro**, pa·**pe**r

   VC·V: **liv·e**r, m**et·a**l, m**ag·i**c, s**ol·e**mn, m**on·a**rch

   NOTE: The letter (x) usually goes with the preceding vowel to form a syllable and usually
   makes that vowel short.

   ex·cite, **ex·**plain

5. A prefix, suffix, or ending with a vowel sound makes a syllable.

   help**·ing**, box**·es**, **re·**do, **un·**lock, slow**·ly**, fast**·er**, play**·ful**, harm**·less**, pain**·ted**, **re·**write

6. When the first vowel in a word is followed by a consonant blend, the blend usually begins the second syllable.

   a·cross, d**e·fr**ost, pr**o·bl**em

7. When the first vowel is followed by a single consonant followed by a consonant blend, the first consonant ends the first syllable and the consonant blend begins the second syllable

   im·prove, h**un·dr**ed, la**un·dr**y, h**am·st**er, s**ur·pr**ise

Evaluation of Syllabication Skills

Ask the child to copy the following words, dividing them into syllables. Have the principles from Activity G-8 available for his/her reference.

1. paper		16. lemon
2. secret		17. boxes
3. toothbrush		18. showing
4. puppet		19. metal
5. longer		20. sudden
6. turtle		21. never
7. apart		22. awful
8. careless		23. fancy
9. already		24. chimney
10. hardly		25. picnic
11. cowboy		26. silver
12. jungle		27. fiddle
13. pencil		28. twenty
14. open		29. Friday
15. hundred		30. thimble

Determining the Number of Syllables

There is a simple way to determine how many syllables in a word. Touch under the chin with the back of a hand. Say the word. Count how many times the chin drops and moves the hand as the word is being spoken. That number tells how many syllables in the word. Show the child this method by saying the following words with him/her and counting the syllables. Children enjoy this activity.

1. laughter   *two*

2. ingredient   *four*

3. emergency   *four*

4. freshwater   *three*

5. wonderful   *three*

6. historic   *three*

7. silvery   *three*

8. embarrass   *three*

9. laundromat   *three*

10. clarinet   *three*

11. frequency   *three*

12. assistant   *three*

If the above words cause problems for the child, practice with two-syllable words first. Later continue with three or four-syllable words. Challenge the child to show where the word would be divided after he/she has determined the number of syllables in the word.

Accented Syllables

In words of more than one syllable, one of the syllables will be pronounced with more emphasis than the others. Tell the child it is stressed or louder than the others. Pronounce the words, neighbor and carpenter, stressing the first syllable. Then pronounce it again stressing the second syllable. Children enjoy hearing the "silly sounding words" when the wrong syllable is stressed.

There are several principles or generalizations about which syllable will be accented or stressed, but as with most generalizations, there will be exceptions. Trial and error is most helpful in finding the accented syllable. Stress first according to principles, but if it does not sound like a word that makes sense, stress another syllable to sound the word.

Principles of Accent:

1. In two-syllable words the first syllable is usually accented.

   hap'•py, Su'•sie, ta'•ble, fin'•ger, prac'•tice, pump'•kin, hun'•gry, break'•fast

2. In most two-syllable words that end in a consonant followed by (y), the first syllable is accented.

   fan'•cy, bug'•gy, ti'•ny, ba'•by, thirst'•y, hun'•gry, hur'•ry

3. The accented syllable will often have a long vowel sound.

   sur•prise', neigh'•bor, pave'•ment, na'•ture

4. The syllable with a schwa sound (when another vowel makes the short (u) sound as in the word up) usually will not be accented.

   pres'•i•dent, **con**•trol', pres'•**ent**, ac'•ci•**dent**
   The syllables that are in bold have the schwa vowel sound.

5. Prefixes, suffixes, and endings (ing, er, est, er,) that form a separate syllable usually are not accented.

   scratch'•ing, bold'•est, faint'•er

6. If the first syllable of a word is (de, re, be, in, im, a, or ex), the first syllable usually will not be accented.

   de•cide', re•turn', re•ward', im•prove', be•tween', in•vite', a•head', ex•plain', be•have', a•bout', a•round', in•stead'

7. The accent usually falls on the root or base word (the part of the word before any suffixes, prefixes, or endings are added).

   fear'•less, part'•ly, bold'•est, cur'•ly, thank'•ful, plain'•ly, camp'•er, pre•ten'•ded

8. If (-tion, -sion, -ture) or (-ment) is the final syllable in a word, it is usually not accented.

   sta'•tion, pic'•ture, mo'•tion, na'•tion, re•fresh'•ment, na'•ture, pave'•ment

9. Some words have a strong accent on one syllable and another syllable accented with less strength. Two syllables are accented, but one is the primary accent and the other is a secondary accent. The primary accented syllable is given more stress. The dictionary marks it with a thicker, darker accent mark.

   grand'•moth'•er, grand'•fa'•ther, (grand is the primary accent) ad'•ver•tise', aer'•o•space', di'•a•gram', e•vap'•o•rate', an'•ti•dote'

Use words that the child knows to teach the principles of accent. Once the child understands the principles, they can be applied to decode unknown words. Work with the examples given above and add others. Pronounce the word emphasizing the accented syllable. Ask the child to tell you what syllable was stressed (strongest, loudest) and discuss which principle or generalization it followed.

Review, Re-teaching, or Evaluation:
Syllables

Use any of the lists of words previously given. After review of the principles for dividing words into syllables in Activity G-8 and accent of syllables in G-11, choose a word and ask the child the following questions. If needed, review vowel sounds in Step C.

How many vowel sounds do you hear in this word?

What vowels make the sounds?

How many syllables are in the word?

Can you divide the word into syllables and tell me why you divided it as you did?

Which syllable(s) is accented?

Made in the USA
Middletown, DE
27 September 2019